312559

D1347658

Falkirk Council

A CHERRYTREE BOOK

This edition first published in 2005
by Cherrytree Books, part of
The Evans Publishing Group Limited
2A Portman Mansions
Chiltern Street
London W1U 6NR

Printed in Italy

British Library Cataloguing in Publication data.

Amos, Janine
Thank You!. – (Good Manners)
1. Interpersonal relations – Juvenile literature
I. Title II. Spenceley, Annabel
395.1'22

ISBN 1 84234 308 4
13 digit ISBN (from January 2007) 978 1 84234 308 1

CREDITS

Editor: Louise John
Designer: Mark Holt
Photography: Gareth Boden
Production: Jenny Mulvanny

Based on the original edition of *Thank You!* published in 1998

With thanks to:
Connor and Amy O'Rourke,
Eileen Morgan, Georgia Rutter,
Frankie Horwood, Megan Tyce,
Samantha Armstrong, Elizabeth Walsingham,
Alyssa Crabb and Nisha Shah

Connor's Birthday

It's Connor's birthday.

4

His friend Amy comes to play.

6

Connor's gran gives him a present.
Connor forgets to say Thank you.

He plays with his friend.
How does Gran feel?

8

Thanks, Gran!

Connor opens his present.
He remembers to say Thank you.

Happy Birthday, Connor.

He gives Gran a hug.

How does Gran feel now?

Making a Rocket

Georgia is making a space rocket.
It's hard work.

13

Her brother Frankie gives her a hand. They build it together.

How do you think Frankie feels?

Georgia shows her big sister.

Georgia thanks Frankie.

How does Frankie feel now?

Elizabeth's Mum

Everyone is playing at Elizabeth's.
Elizabeth's mum gives them juice.

Elizabeth's mum gives them some cakes.

23

It's time to go home.
How is Elizabeth's mum feeling?

25

Elizabeth thinks about it.

Elizabeth thanks her mum.

Thanks for a great time, Mum.

How is Elizabeth's mum feeling now?

It makes them feel warm inside.

Saying thank you shows you're grateful to someone else.

When someone does something for you, don't forget to say...

...thank you!

TEACHER'S NOTES

By reading these books with young children and inviting them to answer the questions posed in the text the children can actively work towards aspects of the PSHE and Citizenship curriculum.

Develop confidence and responsibility and making the most of their abilities by
- recognising what they like and dislike, what is fair and unfair and what is right and wrong
- to share their opinions on things that matter to them and explain their views
- to recognise, name and deal with their feelings in a positive way

Develop good relationships and respecting the differences between people
- to recognise how their behaviour affects others
- to listen to other people and play and work co-operatively
- to identify and respect the differences and similarities between people

EXTENSION ACTIVITY
A game
- Sit the children in a circle. Read through the first story in the book and ask the children to answer the questions posed by the text. At the end of the story ask the children why they think Connor forgot to thank Gran for the present.
- Introduce a game to help everyone remember to say Thank You when someone gives them something. Use an everyday classroom object such as a book or pencil. Pass it to the person on your right and say 'Here is a pencil for you.' They take it and say 'Thank you'. The pencil is passed all the way round the circle this way.
- If anyone forgets to say 'Thank you' the pencil is taken back and given to the person on the other side and the game moves round the circle in the other direction. When the object has gone all round the circle with everybody remembering to say 'Here is a...' and 'Thank you' the last person can choose a new object to start over again.

Discussion
- Remind the children that everything they have was given to them by someone. Ask them if they can identify where some everyday things originate from, such as books in the library, pencils, their clothes, their lunch packs. Answers might include a parent, the school, the government, God or the headteacher. Ask them to think about the different ways they might say thank you for these things.

These drama activities can be repeated on subsequent days with the other two stories in the book or with other stories from the series.